Mount Rainier
National Park

impressions

photography by Charles Gurche

FARCOUNTRY
PRESS

ABOVE: Pasqueflowers and lupine flourish on Naches Peak.

FACING PAGE: Mount Rainier at sunset from Tipsoo Lake.

TITLE PAGE: Lupine and paintbrush below the Tatoosh Range in Mount Rainier National Park.

FRONT COVER: Mount Rainier rising above lupine-filled meadows.

BACK COVER: Comet Falls.

ISBN 10: 1-56037-240-0
ISBN 13: 978-1-56037-240-0

© 2003 by Farcountry Press
Photography © 2003 by Charles Gurche

For more information about our books, write Farcountry Press, P.O. Box 5630, Helena, MT 59604; call (800) 821-3874; or visit www.farcountrypress.com.

Created, produced, and designed in the United States.
Printed in China.

16 15 14 13 12   2 3 4 5 6

ABOVE: Viewing sunrise from Sunset Ridge.

FACING PAGE: Mount Rainier's south face greets the morning.

FOREWORD BY BOB MCINTYRE, JR.

In the early light of dawn a huge white mountain towers over low surrounding hills. All is well as human activity begins. The Mountain is near.

Mount Rainier has been a symbol of power and rugged beauty since before the earliest written records. Thousands of years have elapsed since the North American glacial system melted northward and cleared the way for humans to settle in the Puget Sound area. During that time Mount Rainier and its sister mountains were woven into the spoken lore of the native people. Fundamental life lessons were taught by using mountains as central characters. Our giant mountain, commonly called Mount Tacoma, often played the role of an excitable, tempestuous adventurer among its quieter brethren. Perhaps early residents were more aware of the strength that our silent volcano holds in reserve, than we are today.

Rainier is an independent volcanic peak, near to but separate from the ranges of northwestern mountains. It is much younger than the Cascade Range that runs beside it.

About a million years ago a part of the Pacific Northwest lowlands, once covered by a shallow sea, was raised up and blanketed with volcanic material. Layer upon layer of rock and ash was deposited until an impressive volcanic cone was formed. It reached its maximum height of around 16,000' perhaps 75,000 years ago. The recent eruptions of the last few thousand years have tended to reduce the mountain's height and have left distinct craters at its top. A combination of glacial carving action, steam explosions, and flooding has etched sheer cliffs and deep furrows. These repeated actions have left the distinct and rugged faces that we see today.

We consider Mount Rainier to be an active volcano. True, there are no indicators that a volcanic eruption is brewing. Geologic investigation, however, has shown that there is a different way for the mountain to demonstrate its power. A tremendous flood of water, rock, and silt roared off the mountain about 5,600 years ago. The mudflow, or lahar, followed the path of the White River, burying the area that is now Enumclaw, and continued for many miles downstream. This sort of cement-like mud avalanche is hard to predict. Smaller versions have happened in our lifetime. The word of caution is: seek high ground at the loud roar of an oncoming lahar, an indication that the mountain is upset.

It is easy to think that our mountain has a personality when we learn how pioneers and more recent visitors have interacted with it during the past two centuries.

British Captain George Vancouver first sighted the mountain in 1792. He named the peak Mount Rainier and recorded the event in his ship's log as he explored Puget Sound.

The first person to record a visit to the flanks of the mountain was British Hudson's Bay Company employee William Fraser Tolmie. The young doctor was so attracted by Mount Rainier that he hired Indian guides to take him there in 1833. After successfully passing through the rainforests northwest of the mountain, Dr. Tolmie climbed its lower slopes and, from a nearby peak, saw the glacial splendor of Mount Rainier.

Because Mount Rainier was so difficult to approach, few attempts were made to climb it during the next fifty years. Only two of the early climbing parties, both in 1870, have been recognized as having reached the highest point on the mountain.

In the early 1880s an American surveyor and scientist, Bailey Willis, was hired to search the Carbon River area northwest of the mountain for coal deposits. The coal mining industry was a prime source of fuel at the time, and railroad spur lines connected the mining area with Puget Sound. It was the mountain's higher-elevation slopes, although not a source of coal, that most attracted Willis. His goal was to make the world aware of the alpine beauty of the area, and to have it preserved within a national park. Newspapers, and the scientific and educational communities, supported his purpose. He continued in his mission after leaving Mount Rainier, and was ultimately successful.

The southwest corner of Mount Rainier, the most visited park area today, was extremely inaccessible in the early 1880s. There were no roads, rail lines, or trails leading to that area in 1883. James Longmire, a 63-year-old resident of Yelm, Washington, guided a climbing party to the mountain that year. He and his party called on Indian Henry, a native of the area, to help them reach Mount Rainier from the south. The party made it to the top. More important to Longmire was his discovery of mineral springs in a meadow area later named for him. He laid claim to the meadow and developed a health spa many miles from the nearest community.

During the 1880s and 1890s, the Longmire family built a hotel and packed visitors in over a horse trail. As business increased, the family hired local labor to complete a very rough road into Longmire's Springs. A steep foot-trail and a longer horse-trail were completed from Longmire's to Paradise in cooperation with developers of high-country tent camps. When the news got out in 1895 that two rival Paradise camps were in operation, travel over the poor quality access route increased at an alarming rate.

In the summer of 1897, an outing, attended by more than 200 members of the Portland Mazamas and other mountaineering organizations, converged on Paradise Valley. The few rental tents at Paradise and the meager food supply on hand could not meet the crowd's needs. Broad newspaper coverage of the event reported that nearly a hundred individuals successfully climbed the mountain.

It was 1899 when the signature of President McKinley officially created Mount Rainier National Park, with no funds set aside to pay for employees to protect and maintain it. Public opinion played a key role in demanding better access to the park and better services after arrival. The torture of spending three days on horseback and then finding inadequate accommodations was soon to end.

The task of building a good road to Paradise was assigned to the U.S. Army Corps of Engineers in 1903, and work on the government road began the next year.

By 1904 a rail line had been completed to Ashford. Deluxe passenger service included a twelve-mile wagon ride from the train station to Longmire's Springs.

Travelers brought back news and photographs of unique scenery. Accounts of camping, hiking, and climbing experiences helped sell newspapers and increase the number of people determined to see Mount Rainier from as close as possible.

FACING PAGE: Near Glacier Vista.

A second hotel was opened at Longmire in 1906 by the railroad enterprise that was transporting guests from the Puget Sound hubs of civilization. More than a thousand park visitors were counted that summer.

When the first autos reached Longmire in 1907, it was obvious that easier access would bring more tourists. Better services were needed for the public and their vehicles. The Department of the Interior gave out yearly contracts to barbers and blacksmiths and mountain guides. Lloyd G. Linkletter had a contract for taking photographs in the park. A sales tent next to the road to Paradise made his one of the most successful businesses.

In 1915 the Department of the Interior started a reorganization that gave birth to the National Park Service the next year. A hundred mountaineers hiked the first recorded group journey completely around the mountain, following much of what became the Wonderland Trail.

The yearly visitor count at Mount Rainier National Park soon exceeded 30,000. It was time for park management to have more control over the crazy quilt of services offered. Most services were merged into a single contract awarded to the newly formed Rainier National Park Company.

More rangers were hired. Some directed traffic snarled by road construction, others patrolled the backcountry, and a few natural history specialists became the first park naturalists during the summer seasons. Public campgrounds were constructed for the comfort of campers, and kept them from sleeping in the open meadows. A few artistically designed rustic buildings expanded visitor accommodations and answered the administrative, operational, and housing needs of park personnel.

The park was better organized during the 1920s, when planning for future needs began. In 1929 a road was built to Sunrise, then called Yakima Park, on the mountain's east side. Campgrounds, cabins, and day services were added, but an anticipated hotel was not completed.

The number of visitors to Mount Rainier National Park continued to increase during the economic depression of the 1930s. Additional campgrounds, new restrooms, and an expanded trail system were built and maintained up to the beginning of World War II by Civilian Conservation Corps men. These out-of-work individuals were recruited from every state in the union, organized by the U.S. Army, and brought to work sites where they were most needed. Park personnel trained and supervised them.

ABOVE: The Ohanapecosh River.

FACING PAGE: Above the Nisqually River Valley.

World War II nearly shut down Mount Rainier National Park. Private vehicle use was limited because of rationing imposed on gas and tires. And, when metal parts wore out, there were no replacements available.

During the years of reduced tourist traffic, Mount Rainier was used by the military. Early in the war, Paradise was busy as a training site for Army ski troops that later fought in the snows of north Italy. The uncrowded and peaceful mountain also provided healthful rehabilitation for war-weary service men.

As soon as the war was over, gasoline and new cars were again available. The most popular parts of the park were overrun by visitors on weekends.

In-depth planning of how the park could adjust to growing public needs was begun in the 1950s, with a study to find what new roads, trails, and structures should be built, and what existing structures needed to be replaced. With Congressional approval, new and replacement construction was done to meet the planning known as "Mission 66."

ABOVE: Asters, arnica, and lupine.

FACING PAGE: Tipsoo Lake, with Mount Rainier beyond.

beyond the level of natural healing.

Periodically, staff reevaluates the quantity of backcountry visitor permits that should be issued for a night's stay in each location. In this way a delicate balance between preservation and use is maintained.

The park has expanded its educational role by sharing natural and historical information with the public through the school systems and by way of the Internet at http://www.nps.gov/mora/

More than a century ago Mount Rainier National Park was created to preserve the beauty of a magnificent mountain encompassed by a broad range of natural surroundings. Since then, the number of people traveling to the mountain and setting foot on its trails has increased from a few hundred to about 2,000,000 each year. The park seeks to balance the numbers of visitors at a given time and encourages spreading visits among the many scenic locations.

We are becoming better keepers of our inheritance. It is our responsibility to care for our park and to make

Park planning and analysis expanded. Emphasis on backcountry management was developed in order to preserve park wilderness, most endangered by the crush of too many people. In 1973 a backcountry management plan was created for Mount Rainier National Park. The plan considered the part of the park not developed for public services to be a "wilderness resource." Visitor impact on the wilderness was measured in terms of what is the maximum number of hikers and campers who can make use of an area without damaging it

sure that its beauty and pleasures continue to be available to visitors a century and longer in the future.

In this fast paced world it has become increasingly valuable to be able to experience a mountain wilderness. Lush rainforest, carpeted floral meadows, and brilliant glaciers are icons of Mount Rainier's richness. We can slow our pace and absorb the healing effect of the mountain's gifts as we visit the park, or while we view the beauty shown in these pages. For the moment we are at peace.

ABOVE: Alpine meadows in Mount Rainier National Park.

FACING PAGE: Ghost Lake's shore, piled with driftwood.

RIGHT: Bunchberry grows in the park.

BELOW: Hoary marmots in a "wrestling" match. TOM AND PAT LEESON

FACING PAGE: Emmons Glacier.

ABOVE: Red fox. TOM & PAT LEESON

FACING PAGE: Stevens Canyon sports autumn color.

ABOVE: Clark's nutcracker, first scientifically described by the Lewis and Clark Expedition.
TOM AND PAT LEESON

RIGHT: The National Park Inn at Longmire invites visitors to sit for a spell.

FACING PAGE: Mystical dawn in White River Park, inside Mount Rainier National Park.

ABOVE: Narada Falls rainbow.

FACING PAGE: The sunrise view of Mount Rainier from Alta Vista.

FOLLOWING PAGES: Sky and cloud, rock and snow: the Tatoosh Range.

ABOVE: Van Trump Creek.

FACING PAGE: Paintbrush abloom in Spray Park.

Mount Adams and the Cowlitz Divide
peek their peaks above clouds at dawn.

ABOVE: A mountain goat's silhouette is softened by Pacific Ocean fog. TOM AND PAT LEESON

FACING PAGE: Along the Ohanapecosh River.

BELOW: Lewis's monkeyflower, named for the explorer who first collected it for botanists.

RIGHT: Paradise Lodge nestles naturally into its setting.

RIGHT: A pine marten on the hunt. TOM AND PAT LEESON

BELOW: Golden reflections in Tipsoo Lake.

FACING PAGE: Old-growth forest within the national park.

ABOVE: Luxuriant growth of lupine and paintbrush.

LEFT: The Cowlitz Chimneys.

ABOVE: A black-tailed deer fawn trusting its camouflage for safety.
TOM AND PAT LEESON

RIGHT: Mount Rainier National Park's historic administration building.

FACING PAGE: Deer Creek cascades down the hillside.

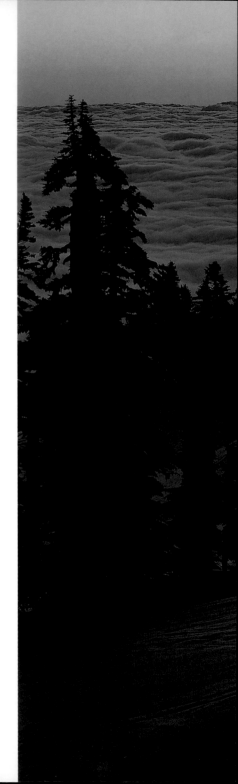

ABOVE: Narada Falls, wearing a winter coat of ice.

RIGHT: Fog mimics snow at dusk on Mount Rainier.

RIGHT: An adult black bear, safe in the park. TOM AND PAT LEESON

BELOW: Closeup study of Douglas-fir.

FACING PAGE: Comet Falls.

ABOVE: Winter swirls over Nisqually Glacier.

FACING PAGE: Chilly sunset, Mount Rainier.

RIGHT: Sunrise Lodge is open from July to mid-October.

BELOW: Spring creeps over the park's alpine meadows.

FACING PAGE: Mount Rainier in Bench Lake.

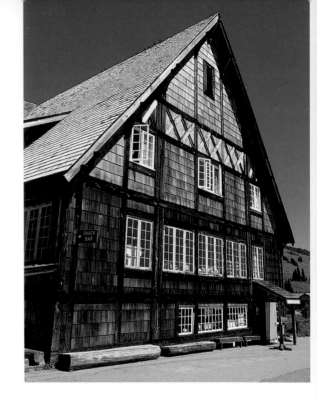

ABOVE: Beneath the Tatoosh Range, huckleberry bushes in autumn red.

FACING PAGE: Martha Falls.

ABOVE: Frozen Lake and Mount Rainier.

FACING PAGE: Spring blossoms beside a snowfield near Glacier Vista.

LEFT: The Carbon River.

BELOW: In the Grove of the Patriarchs are Douglas-firs, Western red cedars and Western hemlocks that were already old in the 11th century.

ABOVE: Stafford Falls.

FACING PAGE: The glories of spring in the Tatoosh.

ABOVE: A bobcat searches for its dinner. TOM AND PAT LEESON

FACING PAGE: Reflection Lake, as touched by hard frost.

LEFT: Looking across the Nisqually River to Mount Rainier.

BELOW: Mount Rainier's glaciers, tinted by sunset.

RIGHT: Golden eagle. TOM AND PAT LEESON

BELOW: Oregon sunshine.

FACING PAGE: Pinnacle Peak.

ABOVE: Eunice Lake reflects Mount Rainier at sunset.

RIGHT: Day's end, viewed from Sourdough Mountain.

ABOVE: Columbia, or tiger lilies are quite common in the park.

LEFT: Storm's end above Cayuse Pass.

ABOVE: Mountain lion. TOM AND PAT LEESON

FACING PAGE: An alpine tarn in Spray Park reflects Mount Rainier.

ABOVE: The view of Mount Rainier from Chinook Pass.

FACING PAGE: Silver Falls.

RIGHT: The Silver Forest's "ghost trees" are survivors of an 1885 wildfire.

BELOW: Longmire Spring was found by James Longmire in 1883, sixteen years before it was included in Mount Rainier National Park.

FACING PAGE: The Paradise Valley filled with shadow.

ABOVE: Ferns deep in the forest.

FACING PAGE: Snow Lake.

ABOVE: Silvery driftwood below Silver Falls.

FACING PAGE: Western pasqueflowers in their seed stage.

ABOVE: Mount Rainier as viewed from Mount Fremont.

FACING PAGE: The beauties of Mount Rainier National Park attract nearly 2 million visitors a year.

ABOVE: Pink mountain heather.

FACING PAGE: A soothing cascade below Mount Rainier.

ABOVE: First light falls on Reflection Lake.

FACING PAGE: Sunrise on Mount Rainier's apex.

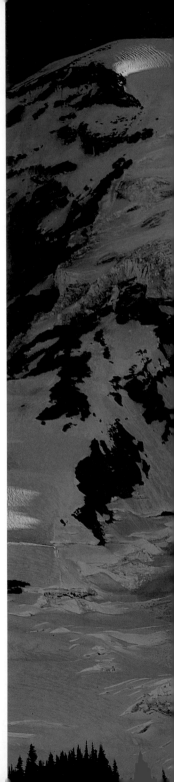

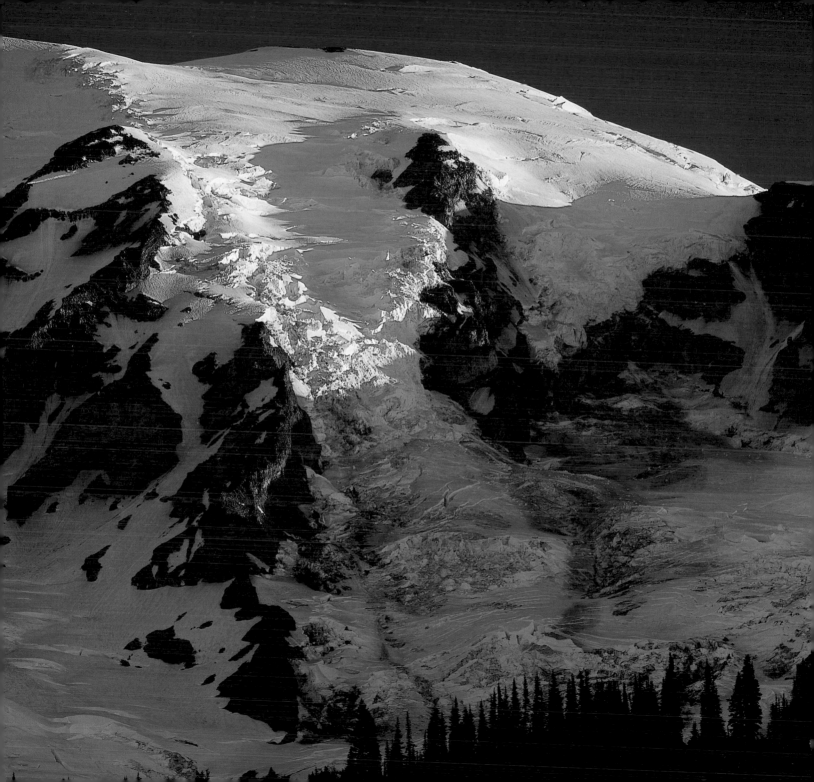

CHARLES GURCHE is one of the United States' foremost nature photographers. His work has appeared in numerous magazines including *Audubon, National Geographic, Natural History,* and *Outside,* and in the books *Missouri Simply Beautiful, Oregon Impressions, Virginia Impressions, Virginia Simply Beautiful* and *Washington Wild and Beautiful.* As sole photographer, he has completed 70 calendars and six books, and has photographed for Kodak, the Sierra Club, Smithsonian Books, and the National Park Service. Awards have been presented to him by the Roger Tory Peterson Institute and the Society of Professional Journalists.